CONNECT WITH
ELECTRICITY

HOW BATTERIES WORK

BY VICTORIA G. CHRISTENSEN

LERNER PUBLICATIONS ◆ MINNEAPOLIS

For my brothers, Joe and Jim, with thanks for
teaching me about electricity
—V.C.

Lerner Publications Company
A division of Lerner Publishing Group, Inc.
241 First Avenue North
Minneapolis, MN 55401 USA

For reading levels and more information, look up this title at
www.lernerbooks.com.

Main body text set in Aptifer Slab LT Pro 12/18.
Typeface provided by Linotype AG.

Library of Congress Cataloging-in-Publication Data

Names: Christensen, Victoria G., author.
Title: How batteries work / by Victoria G. Christensen.
Description: Minneapolis : Lerner Publications, [2016] | Series: Connect with
    electricity | Audience: Ages 8–11. | Audience: Grades 4 to 6. | Includes
    bibliographical references and index.
Identifiers: LCCN 2015041868| ISBN 9781512407815 (lb : alk. paper) |
    ISBN 9781512410068 (pdf)
Subjects: LCSH: Electric batteries—Juvenile literature. | Electricity—Juvenile
    literature. | Electric circuits—Juvenile literature.
Classification: LCC TK2901 .C527 2016 | DDC 621.31/242—dc23

LC record available at http://lccn.loc.gov/2015041868

Manufactured in the United States of America
1-39353-21165-2/29/2016

CONTENTS

NASA's *Curiosity* rover took this selfie on October 31, 2012, while exploring Mars. *Curiosity*'s battery runs on nuclear power. The battery needs to be able to store a lot of energy so *Curiosity* can do its job!

How often do you use a TV remote, a digital camera, or an Xbox One controller? If you use them frequently, then you've probably had to change their batteries. Electronic devices like these require batteries to power them. Have you ever wondered what the plus and minus symbols on a battery mean? Or how something as small as a battery can store so much power?

Batteries do two things: they store energy and they turn chemical energy into electrical energy. The energy stored in a battery can produce light, heat, or motion. Our cell phones, flashlights, and electronic toys would not work without batteries. Beyond household devices, batteries can power huge machines like the *Curiosity* rover on Mars. Batteries of the future might even power self-driving cars!

So let's check out what batteries are made of and how they work. They may seem small, but these little guys make electricity available to us whenever we need it.

CHAPTER ONE

DISCOVERING HOW TO STORE ELECTRICITY

Early scientists wondered if it would be possible to store an electrical charge. After much research, scientists invented batteries to store electricity, which is a form of energy. So to know how batteries work, you need to first know where electricity comes from. It existed long before anyone understood how it worked. To understand electricity and batteries, you have to start with the atom. This tiny bit of matter is too small to see.

Atoms are made up of electrons, protons, and neutrons. The protons and neutrons are at the center, or nucleus, of the atom. Electrons circle the nucleus. At one point scientists believed that the electrons orbit the nucleus like planets orbit the sun, but they now have different theories about how electrons move around the nucleus.

Protons and electrons hold energy in the form of an electrical charge. Electrons have a negative charge, represented with a minus sign, while protons have a positive charge, represented with a plus sign. Neutrons have no charge. Two protons will repel each other and so will two

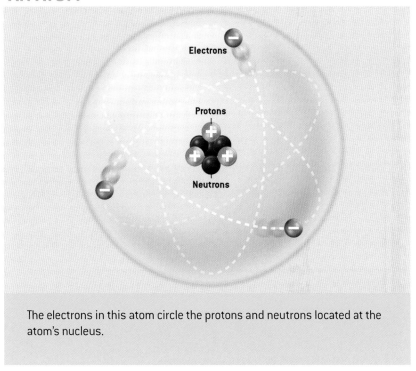

The electrons in this atom circle the protons and neutrons located at the atom's nucleus.

electrons. But protons and electrons are attracted to each other. The electrons are pulled toward the protons in the atom's nucleus. That's why they circle the center.

Atoms start out with the same number of electrons and protons. In other words, the atom is balanced. When an atom loses an electron, it has more positive particles than negative particles. So the atom becomes positively charged and is no longer balanced. Adding an extra electron to an atom makes a negative charge. A negatively charged atom is also unbalanced.

When atoms are unbalanced, electrons move about until they can find a place on an atom. A positively charged atom will look for a free electron to fill the space of a missing electron, and free electrons want to find a spot on an atom.

All matter is made up of atoms—even people and animals. So people and animals have electricity inside their bodies. They use that electricity to send messages throughout their bodies.

ANIMAL ELECTRICITY

Luigi Galvani was an Italian professor, a scientist, and also a medical doctor. During the 1780s, he performed some experiments on animals. He made the legs of dead frogs move by touching

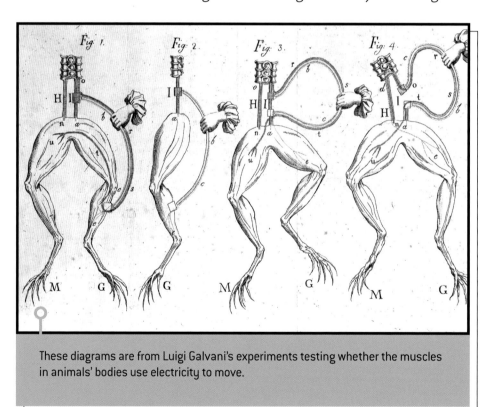

These diagrams are from Luigi Galvani's experiments testing whether the muscles in animals' bodies use electricity to move.

ELECTRIC EELS

Some animals use electricity for defense, such as an electric eel. This fish can create an electric charge. Electric eels live in murky waters and are nearly blind, so they send out electric pulses to help them navigate. They also use electric jolts to stun their prey. This works because their bodies have about six thousand electrocytes, special cells that store power. Cells are the smallest unit of a living organism. Electrocytes are a bit like tiny batteries. When an eel senses danger, the electrocytes discharge about 600 volts—these are the units we use to measure electricity.

them with strips of metal charged with static electricity. His experiment showed that animal movement was based on electricity in some way. His experiments became important to scientists who study how our bodies use electricity to send internal messages.

Scientist Alessandro Volta also studied electricity in the late eighteenth century. When he heard about Galvani's frogs, Volta wondered if their movement was caused by electricity. He wanted to see if a dead frog would move if he touched it with two pieces

FRANKENSTEIN: FACT LEADS TO FICTION

The discovery that electricity could cause muscles to move interested many people. It led author Mary Shelley to write the novel *Frankenstein* in 1816. This book is about a creature made from the body parts of dead people. In the story, an electrical charge from a lightning storm brought the creature to life.

This engraving from Mary Shelley's book illustrates the moment when electricity brings Dr. Frankenstein's monster to life.

of the same metal. It did not. He found out that he needed two different metals to make a frog move. Using two different metals was important because each metal had a different electrical charge, meaning their charges were not equal to one another. The charges from the two metals needed to balance, or equalize. When the free electrons traveled to find open atoms, this caused the flow of electricity, and the frog's legs moved. He discovered that frogs weren't electric. Their bodies just acted as paths for an electric current.

THE FIRST MODERN BATTERY

Volta found that by connecting different pairs of metals, he could make stronger electric currents. This gave him the idea for a battery. In his design, Volta stacked metal plates made from silver and zinc, alternating the two kinds of metal. The plates were each separated by a thick paper card that had been soaked in salt water. Salt water is good for conducting electricity because it allows electrons in the water to move freely. Volta's invention was called the voltaic pile. The voltaic pile and the volt were named after Volta to honor his discoveries.

Volta's battery supplied a steady flow of electricity, which meant that it could be used to power other devices that use electricity. Without Volta's invention, there could be no cell phones, remote-control cars, or flashlights. Can you imagine modern life without batteries?

CHAPTER TWO

DESIGNING BATTERIES

Scientists and engineers go through a process when they design something new. First, they identify the problem, or what they're trying to do with their new design. Second, they brainstorm ideas. Sometimes this means talking it over with other scientists. They might come up with really wild ideas, ideas that might sound impossible to other scientists. Next, scientists start to design. They may sketch their plans on paper, though modern engineers often design on a computer. Then they build and test their designs to see what works and what doesn't. This might lead to a redesign, if their first ideas don't work perfectly. Design ideas don't always work the way they're supposed to on the first try. That means more building and testing. Once they have found a design that works, they share their solution with others.

Alessandro Volta studied more about electricity than just how it flowed through animals and metal plates. He wanted to find out how static electricity could be stored. He had been thinking of inventing a long-distance communication device, wondering if it was possible to send an electric signal through a wire strung up from one town in Italy to another. To do this, he first

THE ENGINEERING METHOD

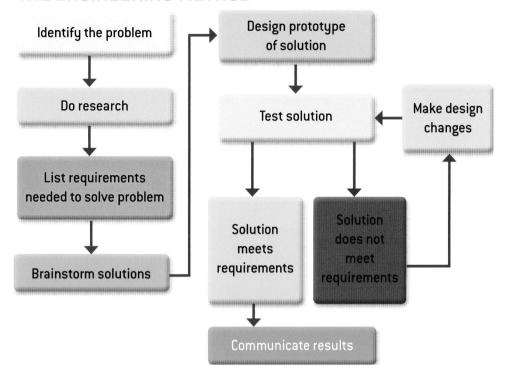

Identify the problem → Do research → List requirements needed to solve problem → Brainstorm solutions → Design prototype of solution → Test solution → Solution meets requirements / Solution does not meet requirements → Make design changes → Communicate results

This diagram shows one way engineers identify and solve a problem, but everyone does it a bit differently. The process can change through the years, so it may not exactly match what Volta and others did in the past.

needed a device that could store electric energy on the other end of the wire so that the signal could be received.

Volta's challenge was to figure out how to capture and store electrical energy. He had tested different ways to move and store electricity. In one design, he used pieces of silver and zinc in rows of cups of acid. If one cup held a silver piece, the next cup held a zinc piece, and so on. The silver or zinc pieces in the cups were connected by metal strips. To test this lineup, he put a finger in each of the cups on the ends of the row and knew his experiment worked when he felt a shock in his finger. In combining the acid and the metals, he had changed chemical energy to electrical energy. One of the chemical reactions created from the acid and metal released electrons, which flowed down the line.

When Volta placed his fingers into the end cups, he completed a circuit, so the electrons were free to flow into his body. But this

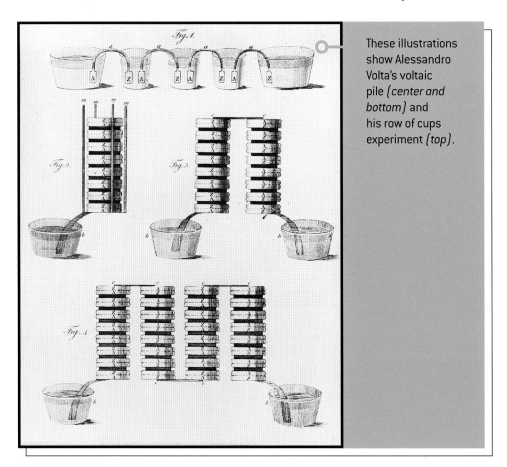

These illustrations show Alessandro Volta's voltaic pile *(center and bottom)* and his row of cups experiment *(top)*.

A STRIKING DISCOVERY

In 1752 Benjamin Franklin wanted to test if lightning was a form of electricity. He knew that lightning often struck tall buildings, but there were no tall buildings in the United States at the time. So he made a kite, attached a small piece of metal wire to the top of it, tied a key to the bottom of the kite string, and flew the kite high off the ground. The metal wire attracted the lightning, which traveled down the wet string to the key. He confirmed that lightning was a form of electricity when he received an electrical shock on his finger from the key.

design wasn't very practical. The acid could spill or very strong shocks could hurt someone, so Volta rethought his design. That rethinking and his experiments with the dead frogs led him to the voltaic pile. In 1800 Volta shared his discovery. He was even invited to show his discovery to Napoleon, the leader of France, in 1801. While he never did build his communication device between the two Italian towns, his discoveries turned out to be extremely useful to modern technology.

CHAPTER THREE

THE PARTS OF A BATTERY

Have you ever noticed the parts of a battery? A battery may be a round cylinder, with a small piece of metal on each end. The metal pieces are called terminals. A rectangular battery may have two terminals on the same end. Batteries come in many shapes and sizes, but in addition to the two terminals on the outside, batteries all have three main parts on the inside: an anode, a cathode, and an electrolyte.

A battery needs all three parts to work. Each part is made up of different chemicals. These can be liquid chemical mixtures or dry paste mixtures or metals. The anode and the cathode are conductors—they allow electricity to travel through them. The electrolyte is a chemical mixture that separates the anode and

Batteries all have the same three parts, but batteries can come in several different shapes and sizes. These differences are based on the amount of electricity the battery can produce.

the cathode so they don't touch each other. When the cathode and anode are connected to an electronic device, the electrolyte starts a reaction. This allows the stored chemical energy to convert to electrical energy.

Have you seen the plus and minus signs on a battery? These signs are on the battery's terminals, which connect to the load. The *load* is a term that engineers use for the electronic device the battery is supposed to power. An example of a load is a flashlight or a camera. A plus sign means it is the positive terminal. The cathode connects

HOW A BATTERY WORKS

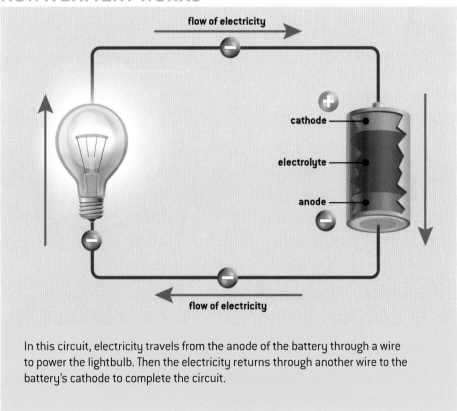

In this circuit, electricity travels from the anode of the battery through a wire to power the lightbulb. Then the electricity returns through another wire to the battery's cathode to complete the circuit.

to the positive terminal. The minus is for the negative terminal. It connects to the anode.

When both terminals are connected to a load, chemical reactions happen inside the battery. The chemical reactions cause a buildup of electrons at the anode. Then the anode has more electrons than the cathode. Because electrons repel one another, they try to move to a place with fewer electrons.

The only place for the electrons to go is to the cathode, but the electrolyte keeps them from going straight through the battery. They must move outside the battery and through the wire that connects the two terminals. This whole connection makes a circuit, where the electrons travel from the anode, outside the battery through the wire, and then back into the battery through the cathode. If the circuit includes a device such as a lightbulb, the bulb will brighten as the electrons travel their path.

FRUITY BATTERIES

Did you know that batteries can be made from fruit? Lemons, oranges, and apples work well as batteries. The juice inside the fruit acts as the electrolyte to control the flow of electricity. Two different metals pushed into the fruit act as the anode and the cathode. Then these metals must be connected with wires to a load, like a lightbulb, to complete the circuit. If you don't have any fruit, vegetables will do. Students often experiment with powering a lightbulb with a potato in science class.

The flow of electricity changes the chemicals in the anode and the cathode. There is a limit to the amount of energy available in a battery, so eventually the anode will run out of electrons. When all the electrons have flowed from one terminal to the other, the battery is discharged. This is what happens when we say a battery dies.

All batteries eventually die, but some batteries can be recharged with electricity from an electrical outlet. In the usual chemical reaction, electrons flow from the negative end of the battery, through the load to the positive end of the battery. When a battery is recharged, the load is replaced by a power source, reversing the usual reaction. This restores the anode and the cathode so that the battery can again provide energy. If a battery can't be plugged into a wall socket, sometimes people use solar power to recharge it. The average rechargeable battery can be reused one thousand times!

SOLVE IT!

RECHARGING DEAD BATTERIES

Imagine you're on an island far away from home. Your battery-operated radio just ran out of power. Since there are no wall outlets, you can't just plug in your radio or your batteries to recharge them. What energy source could you use to recharge the batteries? What tools might you need to take advantage of that power source? *(Answer key is on page 35.)*

CHAPTER FOUR

CURRENTS AND CIRCUITS

Currents and circuits are important to batteries and electronic devices. An electric current is the flow of electrons. The battery supplies the energy so an electric current can flow through a circuit.

CURRENTS

There are two main types of current: direct and alternating. Direct current (DC) is produced by batteries. It allows electric current to flow constantly in one direction. The electrons move from atom to atom only in that direction. Most handheld games and toys use DC, getting their power directly from a battery.

DC is different from the current that comes from an electrical outlet in your home. The electricity that runs through a house or apartment building is called alternating current (AC). With AC, the electrical charge constantly changes, or alternates, directions. The electrons move from atom to atom in one direction for a

This boy's handheld game is powered by the direct current that comes from batteries.

21

while, but then they turn around and move in the other direction. In other words, the electrons in AC move back and forth.

AC is not produced by batteries, but it can be used to charge batteries that have died after the AC is converted to DC. AC flows through most power lines. The voltage from the AC power running through your home can be very dangerous, so if you want to experiment with electricity, stick to DC. You should never do any experiments with a household electrical outlet.

MAD SCIENTIST

Nikola Tesla was an engineer who studied AC in the late nineteenth and early twentieth centuries. He was at odds with Thomas Edison, who favored DC. Tesla may have been right about the power of AC, but he also came up with lots of wild ideas, such as a death ray. He also talked about heating the night sky with wireless electrical power and collecting the sun's energy using an antenna. These ideas didn't seem possible to people back in the 1930s and may still seem strange. But he also talked about a global wireless communication system, and modern people communicate worldwide via the Internet. Perhaps not all of his ideas were so strange after all.

Nikola Tesla's induction motor was an electric motor that used alternating current.

CIRCUITS

The path electricity flows along is called a circuit. The components, or parts, of a circuit are joined by wires. In a simple circuit, electricity flows in a complete circle without branching off to take another route. To work, an electric circuit needs a power source and the circuit needs to be closed. This means that the wires connecting all the switches, lightbulbs, and any other parts must start and end at the battery, the power source. If any part of the circuit is not connected, electricity won't flow. The positive and negative ends of a battery cause the current to flow all the way around the circuit.

A SIMPLE CIRCUIT

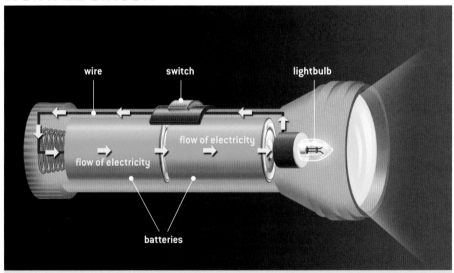

This flashlight is powered by a simple circuit. Electricity travels from the batteries to the lightbulb and the power switch through a wire, which connects them back to the batteries. When you turn the switch, or power button, to Off on a flashlight, you disconnect the circuit and electricity can no longer flow.

Series circuits and parallel circuits are more complicated. A series circuit is a circuit with no branches, or routes for electricity to flow outside the main circuit. When you watch a television series, there are many episodes, one after another. A series circuit is similar in that there are several components, one after another, along the same wire. A lightbulb is an example of a component. If you add more lights to a series circuit, each light will become dimmer because the current through the series circuit decreases when the voltage is divided among all the lightbulbs. If one light breaks in a series circuit, the whole circuit is broken and all the lights will stop working.

SERIES CIRCUIT

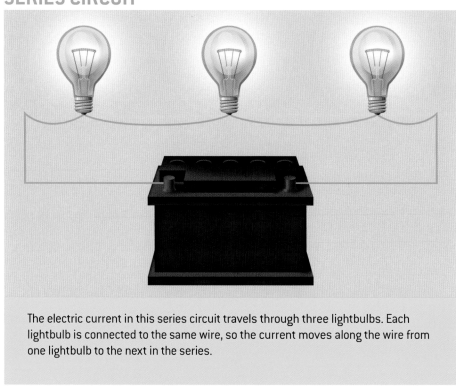

The electric current in this series circuit travels through three lightbulbs. Each lightbulb is connected to the same wire, so the current moves along the wire from one lightbulb to the next in the series.

Strings of holiday lights used to be built using series circuits. If a light burned out or broke, the whole string of lights stopped working. To solve this problem, many holiday lights are built with parallel circuits or a combination of series and parallel circuits.

In a parallel circuit, components are connected on different branches of the wire, providing multiple paths for the electricity to follow. If one light goes out, the remaining lights stay lit because

PARALLEL CIRCUIT

There are three lightbulbs in this parallel circuit. They're connected to a wire that breaks off into three different branches, or sections, so the electric current can travel to each lightbulb at once instead of traveling to the lightbulbs in order.

electricity can follow one of the other paths. A light stays bright even if you add more lights to the parallel circuit. This is because the voltage to each light stays the same. Homes and other buildings are wired with parallel circuits. Even if one component in a parallel circuit breaks, the rest will still work.

A switch breaks the flow of current through a circuit. For example, you don't have to wait until the battery runs out to turn off your flashlight. You can flip a switch by pressing the Off button to stop the current. When the switch is in the On position, the circuit is closed and electricity can flow. When the switch is in the Off position, there is a gap in the circuit. Because you opened the circuit, the electrons are stopped in their tracks.

We don't always want every light or electric appliance turned on at once in our home. Parallel circuits are useful when we only want to use certain electronics at a given time.

Sometimes a circuit is bypassed and the electricity finds a different path to follow. This is called a short circuit. The electricity doesn't necessarily take a shorter course, just an easier one. A short circuit can happen when a bare wire crosses another wire. For example, you might drop your flashlight and the wires inside are knocked out of place. The electricity flows through a wire path that wasn't intended for it. When this happens, your flashlight might go out. The insulation around wires inside the walls of a house may decay, allowing bare wires to come into contact with each other when they shouldn't. This can also create a short circuit. If the energy intended for a light or appliance travels through a short circuit, the currents can cause the wires to get hot, which might even start a fire.

SOLVE IT!

ELECTRON TRAFFIC JAM

Imagine that electrons are like cars moving along a road, like a circuit. The cars are in a parking lot at a busy stadium after a football game, and all the fans want to go to a shopping mall that has lots of restaurants. All the cars are trying to leave at the same time. The parking lot has only one exit, and only one road leads to the mall. If there is an accident, all these cars would need to stop. If you thought of this idea in terms of circuits and electrons, would this circuit be a series circuit or a parallel circuit? How could this scenario change to represent the other kind of circuit? *(Answer key is on page 35.)*

CHAPTER FIVE

CAR BATTERIES

People use cars to get to work, school, and other places. Most modern cars get their energy from burning gasoline, but electric cars use electricity to run and other cars called hybrids use a combination of gas and electricity. Energy is stored in these cars' batteries. From the outside, electric cars look almost the same as gas cars. One big difference is that an electric car has no tailpipe. It doesn't need it because it has no gas exhaust. But on the inside, it's a different story—especially the battery.

The main difference between a gas car battery, a hybrid car battery, and an electric car battery is its function. A gas car battery is there mainly to start the gasoline engine. After the engine has been started, gas is used to keep the car moving down the road. A hybrid car battery starts the gas engine *and* helps the engine move the car down the road. An electric car battery does not have a gasoline engine that must be started, so this type of battery just keeps the car moving down the road.

A gas car battery works when an electric circuit is connected to the battery, allowing electrons to flow. The gas car battery works the same way as other batteries—it has a cathode, an anode, and an electrolyte that convert chemical energy into electrical energy. But

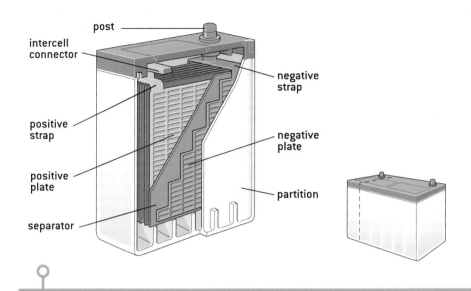

label: post
label: intercell connector
label: negative strap
label: positive strap
label: negative plate
label: positive plate
label: partition
label: separator

This diagram shows the inside of one gas car battery, or cell, on the left. On the right is the battery you'd typically see under a car's hood. Six of the cells are packed together in a case.

a gas car battery is really six small batteries. These small batteries, sometimes called cells, are packed neatly inside a case, so you only see what appears to be one big battery. The cells are lined up in a series. Remember the series circuit? Because the cells are in a series, the voltage of each cell is added together. So if each cell is 2 volts and there are six cells, there are 12 volts. It takes 12 volts to start the car.

We sometimes call the gas car battery a lead-acid battery because of the chemicals that are inside it. An electric car can run with a lead-acid battery, but it won't get very far. Engineers are still working on better batteries for electric cars. Because an electric car battery runs the car's motor, it has to be much more powerful than the battery in a gas car, which only starts the car.

Engineers have designed more powerful batteries by using different chemicals inside them. These batteries have high energy density. This means they can store a lot more chemical energy than a lead-acid battery. Like all batteries, electric car batteries also have an anode, a cathode, and an electrolyte. But some bigger electric cars have batteries that can create up to 650 volts—that's much more than the 12 volts of a gas car battery.

RECHARGING ELECTRIC CARS

Batteries in electric cars need be recharged when they run out of electricity. People plug in electric and hybrid cars at home or at recharging stations. The driving range of electric cars is about 50 to 150 miles (80 to 241 kilometers). Then drivers have to stop to recharge the battery. Sometimes electric car owners find it hard to find a place to plug in their car while they are on a trip. We already have electricity at most locations along highways, but we need more charging stations in parking lots and other areas where they are accessible to electric cars. We also need batteries that can be charged more quickly—maybe about five minutes—about how long it takes for a gasoline car to be filled with a tank of gas.

This Nissan Leaf is a fully electric car. Its battery pack is the orange piece under the seats.

CHAPTER SIX

FUTURE TECHNOLOGY

*S*pirit and *Opportunity* landed on Mars in 2004 to explore the planet. They use electricity to collect data about the planet and send it back to scientists on Earth. Just as batteries are useful for so many modern electronic devices, they will continue to help advance science and technology of the future. The more powerful batteries become, the more we'll be able to do with them.

MARS ROVERS

Scientists and engineers have recently needed to address the limits of solar energy. Satellites and rovers bring us information from outer space, and their batteries are recharged with solar energy. In the early twenty-first century, NASA engineers built two space rovers called *Spirit* and *Opportunity*. They have solar panels, which collect energy from sunlight and convert that energy to electricity for a device's batteries.

Solar panels are made up of solar cells. A solar cell is made from two layers of silicon, an element that is used in many electronics. Chemicals are added to the bottom layer that cause it to have more protons than electrons, while the top layer has more electrons than protons. When the sun shines on the cell, the energy knocks the electrons from the top layer to the bottom layer. This causes the electrons in the lower layer to move up through a wire to the top layer, creating a current and starting the flow of electricity.

Engineers had hoped these rovers could continue to gather energy from the sun on their travels around Mars. For one rover, the plan worked. *Opportunity* was still exploring Mars in 2016. But *Spirit* ran out of power. It sits on the dark side of Mars, so no sunlight can reach its solar panels. Because *Spirit* uses a solar-powered battery, it cannot be recharged. Scientists used what they learned from this test to design a new rover named *Curiosity*. Its battery is nuclear-powered instead of solar-powered, so it can store a lot more energy and doesn't need the sun as an energy source. Without relying on the sun as an energy source, the rover's designers hope it won't lose power if it travels to the dark side of Mars.

SELF-DRIVING CARS

In the future, we might have electric cars that are self-driving. Some car companies have been testing self-driving cars already. These cars have a computer to collect data from cameras and sensors. The computer helps the car stay on the road. These cars can't do everything a person can, but they can watch all sides of a car at the same time. Engineers are even working on cars that might someday talk to one another. These cars would need powerful batteries. Scientists and engineers will need to design batteries that can store much more energy. A powerful battery like this might

32

This self-driving car takes its passenger down a California road. The bulb on the top of the car contains all of the sensors, radars, and cameras that the car uses to see where it is going and what is near it.

be too heavy for the car though, so engineers will need to consider a design to make these powerful batteries smaller as well.

It's hard to imagine living without batteries. Batteries have completely changed how we live. Without batteries there would be no flashlights, handheld games, or cell phones. Can you imagine what it would be like to go camping with only candlelight? Without the batteries used in cars and buses, some kids would have to find another way to get to school. Many of the things we use every day have batteries, and devices of the future will too.

STATIC ELECTRICITY

Test your knowledge of electricity and the movement of electrons. You can be a scientist like Luigi Galvani and experiment with static electricity—but without the frogs! In this experiment, you'll use a balloon to move an empty soda can without touching the can yourself. How can you use static electricity to move the can? Does a bigger balloon work better or a smaller one? Brainstorm ideas for how you might move the can.

WHAT YOU'LL NEED

- two balloons
- an empty soda can
- a head of hair or a wool sweater

WHAT YOU'LL DO

1. Blow up each of the balloons, either with your breath or with a balloon pump. One balloon should be larger than the other. Ask an adult if you need assistance with this.
2. Think about what you have learned about electricity and the movement of electrons. Put the can on its side on a table or a smooth floor. Rub one of the balloons back and forth on your hair or sweater really fast.
3. Hold the balloon close to the can without actually touching the can. What happens?
4. Then try using the other balloon. Did one balloon work better than the other?

FOLLOW-UP

1. Were you able to predict what would happen when you pushed the balloon toward the can?
2. When you rubbed a balloon on your hair, electrons built up on the surface of the balloon. This was static electricity. Thinking back to what you've learned about electricity and an electron's charge, why do you think the balloons pushed the can away?

RECHARGE DEAD BATTERIES (PAGE 20)

The easiest way to recharge your batteries on a faraway island is probably solar power. Scientists and engineers often use solar-powered batteries when they are working in very remote places. Solar panels are part of many instruments or even part of a battery itself. If your radio has regular batteries that are not solar powered, you could pack a lightweight solar-powered battery charger.

ELECTRON TRAFFIC JAM (PAGE 27)

The first example, with only one road, is like a series circuit. If there were many open roads available between the stadium and the mall, the cars could take different paths. This is like a parallel circuit, because there are many possible pathways for the cars (or electrons) to follow. If there was an accident on one road, cars might take another.

atom: the smallest unit of any substance. It is made up of a positively charged center surrounded by electrons.

chemical: a substance that is used to make a change to atoms or molecules

chemical energy: energy stored in atoms and molecules. Chemical energy is released in a chemical reaction.

circuit: a closed path through which electricity flows

conductor: a substance through which electricity travels

electric current: the movement of electricity

electrocyte: a special muscle or nerve cell in a person or animal that generates electricity

electrolyte: the chemical in a battery that helps control the change from chemical energy into electrical energy

electron: the part of an atom with a negative electrical charge

energy: fuel or electricity used for power

load: an electrical component that is powered by electricity

power source: an electrical component that supplies electrical power

static electricity: an electrical charge that collects on the surfaces of some objects

terminal: a point where a connection can be made to an electrical circuit

volt: a unit that measures the strength of an electrical current

voltage: the potential difference in charge between two points in an electrical field

SELECTED BIBLIOGRAPHY

Beiser, Arthur. *Physics.* 5th ed. Reading, MA: Addison-Wesley, 1992.

Bodanis, David. *Electric Universe: The Shocking True Story of Electricity.* New York: Crown, 2005.

Brain, Marshall. *The Engineering Book: From the Catapult to the Curiosity Rover; 250 Milestones in the History of Engineering.* New York: Sterling, 2015.

Coulson, C. A., and T. J. M. Boyd. *Electricity.* 2nd ed. New York: Longman, 1979.

Franklin, Benjamin. *Benjamin Franklin: The Autobiography and Other Writings.* Edited by Kenneth Silverman. New York: Penguin, 1986.

Woodford, Chris, Luke Collins, Clint Witchalls, Ben Morgan, and James Flint. *Cool Stuff and How It Works.* London: DK, 2005.

LERNER
SOURCE

Expand learning beyond the printed book. Download free, complementary educational resources for this book from our website, www.lerneresource.com.

FURTHER INFORMATION

Battery Kids
https://www.chromebattery.com/battery-kids
Visit this website to learn more about batteries and explore different science experiments you can try at home or school.

Energy Kids
http://www.eia.gov/kids/index.cfm
Explore this government site about sources of energy and scientists who made energy discoveries. Then play some energy games and do some activities!

Frankenstein's Lightning Laboratory
http://www.miamisci.org/af/sln/frankenstein/safety.html
Learn about electrical safety at this fun and interactive website.

How Do Batteries Work?
http://mocomi.com/how-do-batteries-work
Visit this site to see how electrons travel through a circuit, from the anode to the cathode of a battery, and see what happens when a battery dies.

McGregor, Harriet. *Electricity*. New York: Windmill Books, 2011.
Read this book and learn more about electricity, circuits, and switches.

Platt, Charles. *Make: Electronics*. 2nd ed. San Francisco: Maker Media, 2015.
Read more about different types of batteries and what part they play in electronics.

Potato Battery
http://pbskids.org/zoom/activities/phenom/potatobattery.html
Check out this web page to learn how to conduct your own potato battery experiment!

Walker, Sally M. *Investigating Electricity*. Minneapolis: Lerner Publications, 2012.
Learn more about how electric current flows through a battery and how to construct your own homemade battery.

INDEX

PHOTO ACKNOWLEDGMENTS

The images in this book are used with the permission of: © iStockphoto.com/da-vooda (electronic icon); © iStockphoto.com/Kubkoo (color dots background); © iStockphoto.com/alenaZ0509 (zigzag background); © iStockphoto.com/Sashatigar (robots and electrical microschemes); NASA/JPL-Caltech/Malin Space Science Systems, p. 4; Rob Schuster, pp. 7, 17, 23, 24, 25; © Wellcome Library, London/Wikimedia Commons (CC BY 4.0), pp. 8, 14; © age fotostock/SuperStock, p. 9; British Library/The Granger Collection, New York, p. 10; © Luigi Chiesa/Wikimedia Commons (CC BY-SA 3.0), p. 11; Independent Picture Service, p. 13; © iStockphoto.com/scanrail, p. 16; © US Army National Guard photo by Staff Sgt. Jerry Saslav, Massachusetts National Guard Public Affairs/flickr.com (CC BY-ND 2.0), p. 18; © SPL/Science Source, p. 19; Andersen Ross/Blend Images/Newscom, p. 21; © Science and Society/SuperStock, p. 22; © iStockphoto.com/Ivan Stevanovic, p. 26; Encyclopædia Britannica/UIG Universal Images Group/Newscom, p. 29; © iStockphoto.com/Sjoerd van der Wal, p. 30; Karl Mondon/TNS/Newscom, p. 33.

Cover: © iStockphoto.com/Diabluses (flashlight); © iStockphoto.com/da-vooda (electronic icon); © iStockphoto.com/Kubkoo (color dots background); © iStockphoto.com/alenaZ0509 (zigzag background); © iStockphoto.com/Sashatigar (robots and electrical microschemes).